The Official Book of Doctor Doctor Jokes

by Andrew Madden

ISBN 978-1-312-89115-9

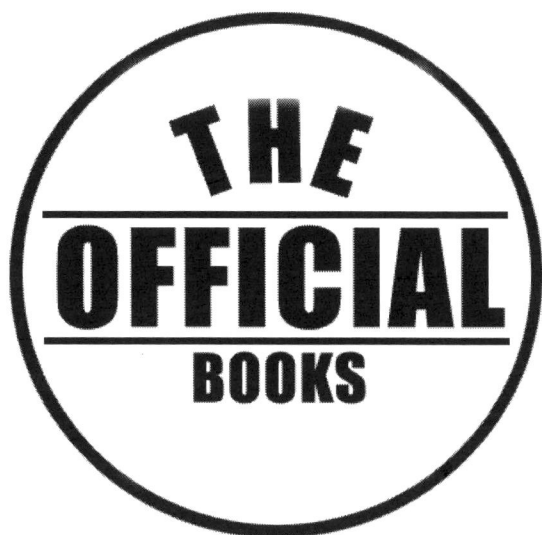

The Book and Author

The Official Book of Doctor Doctor Jokes is the creation of Andrew Madden, a part-time writer, artist and family comedian. It was just one day whilst looking for jokes on the internet that he had the impulse, after seeing the same Doctor Doctor jokes over and over again, to come up with a whole new range of jokes. After writing his first joke, more and more came almost naturally until he ended up with the huge collection that you find before you in this book!

The book contains over 200 doctor doctor jokes in total, some classic one's, some re-written and over **100 brand new jokes** written by the author. All jokes follow the traditions of doctor doctor jokes meaning that the jokes are mostly good-natured and some, of course, a little naughty, but most importantly all are **side-splittingly funny!**

Contents

The Collection

Doctor Doctor, my wife hit me on the neck with a sieve ...

Oh, did you strain it?

Andrew Madden

Doctor Doctor, my hair's going grey but I'm allergic to hair colourings ...

Don't worry, you won't dye.

Andrew Madden

Doctor Doctor, my teeth keep falling out ...

Don't worry, we'll soon get to the root of the problem.

Andrew Madden/Anon

Doctor Doctor, I keep thinking parts of me are invisible ...

Yes, you're definitely not all there.

Andrew Madden/Anon

Doctor Doctor, I keep thinking about cows teats ...

You sound udderly confused.

Andrew Madden/Anon

Doctor Doctor, I keep thinking that I'm a naughty bumblebee ...

Oh sit down on your beehind and beehive!

Andrew Madden

Doctor Doctor, I'm really bad at telling Chemistry jokes ...

Why's that?

I can never get any reaction.

Andrew Madden/Anon

Doctor Doctor, my hair's falling out. I need something to keep it in ...

OK, here's an old shoe box.

Anon

Doctor Doctor, I think I'm addicted to brake fluid ...

Don't be silly. You can stop at any time.

Andrew Madden/Anon

Doctor Doctor, every time I have a cup of tea I get a stabbing pain in my eye ...

Try taking the spoon out first.

Anon

17

Doctor Doctor, I feel like a sheep ...

Oh, that's baaaaaaaaaad.

Anon

Doctor Doctor, I think I need glasses ...

Yes, so do I. This is a shoe shop.

Andrew Madden/Anon

Doctor Doctor, I don't want to talk to you about my study on the fear of hedgehogs ...

Why not? Is it a prickly subject?

Andrew Madden

Doctor Doctor, I think I'm a dancing composer ...

Wait. I'll be Bach in a Minuet.

Andrew Madden/Anon

Doctor Doctor, since my wife and I bought our matching waterbeds, our relationship has never been the same ...

Oh, are you drifting apart?

Andrew Madden

Doctor Doctor, I'm in denial ...

Really? I thought you were in-Seine.

Andrew Madden

Doctor Doctor, keep thinking I'm a bell ...

Take these. If you don't feel better tomorrow give me a ring.

Andrew Madden/Anon

Doctor Doctor, I got dropped from the cricket team. They call me butterfingers ...

Don't worry, it's not catching.

Anon

Doctor Doctor, I'm really worried about my breathing ...

Don't worry, we'll soon put a stop to that!

Anon

Doctor Doctor, I've got acute appendicitis ...

Yes, I agree. Your liver looks lovely too.

Andrew Madden/Anon

Doctor Doctor, what can you give me for wind? ...

Here, try this kite.

Anon

Doctor Doctor, my relationship with my boyfriend with the wooden leg is over ...

Oh, did you break it off?

Andrew Madden

Doctor Doctor, another doctor said I should put goose fat all over my back ...

If you do that you'll go downhill fast.

Anon

Doctor Doctor, I've become a kleptomaniac ...

Have you taken anything for it?

So far a sofa, three TV's and a necklace.

Anon

Doctor Doctor, you said I'd be dead in ten. Ten what? Years? Months? ...

Ten, nine, eight, ...

Anon

Doctor Doctor, I injured myself whilst tap dancing ...

Oh, did you fall into the sink?

Andrew Madden/Anon

Doctor Doctor, I keep losing my memory ...

When did this first happen?

When did what first happen?

Anon

Doctor Doctor, I have water on the brain. What do you recommend? ...

A tap on the head.

Andrew Madden/Anon

Doctor Doctor, I keep imagining that I'm an escaped fortune telling dwarf ...

So, a small medium at large.

Andrew Madden/Anon

Doctor Doctor, I always forget the most important thing when making pants ...

Yes, sew it seams.

Andrew Madden

Doctor Doctor, I can't stop my hands shaking ...

Do you drink a lot?

No, I spill most of it!

Anon

Doctor Doctor, I'm so tired of my job at the IRS/HMRC ...

Why? Is it too taxing?

Andrew Madden

Doctor Doctor, I snore so loud that I keep myself awake ...

Sleep in another room then.

Anon

Doctor Doctor, I'm having trouble at my job at the orange juice factory ...

Why's that?

I just can't concentrate.

Andrew Madden/Anon

Doctor Doctor, I'm afraid of juggling ...

Why's that?

I just don't have the balls to do it.

Andrew Madden/Anon

Doctor Doctor, I believe I'm a Harry Potter character ...

Are you Sirius?

Andrew Madden

Doctor Doctor, I can only use the elevator ...

Why's that?

I feel the stairs are always up to something.

Andrew Madden/Anon

Doctor Doctor, I believe that I'm a koala ...

That's a bit fur-fetched. In fact it's bearly believable.

Andrew Madden

Doctor Doctor, I feel like a carrot ...

Don't get yourself in a stew.

Anon

Doctor Doctor, I'm devoid of any emotion ...

How do you feel about that?

Andrew Madden

Doctor Doctor, I've swallowed my pocket-money ...

Take this then we'll see if there's any change in the morning.

Anon

Doctor Doctor, I'm addicted to visiting different shopping centres ...

There's no need. Once you've seen one shopping centre you've seen a-mall.

Andrew Madden/Anon

Doctor Doctor, I'm at deaths' door ...

Don't worry, we'll soon pull you through.

Anon

Doctor Doctor, as a quarterback, sometimes I feel that if I throw so many times I'll die ...

There's really no need to worry. Just pass away.

Andrew Madden

Doctor Doctor, my spouse is so ill. Is there no hope? ...

It depends on what you're hoping for.

Anon

Doctor Doctor, I'm worried about my shape ...

Don't worry, there a 6 million people just like you, but those are just round figures.

Andrew Madden/Anon

Doctor Doctor, help me quickly! I'm getting shorter and shorter! ...

Just wait there and be a little patient.

Anon

Doctor Doctor, this blood test report says that I'm type-A ...

Oh sorry. That's a type-O.

Andrew Madden/Anon

Doctor Doctor, my nose runs and my feet smell ...

I fear you may have been built upside-down.

Anon

Doctor Doctor, I got fired from my job at the calendar making factory ...

Why's that?

I took an extra day off.

Andrew Madden

Doctor Doctor, I've got a little bit of lettuce sticking out of my bottom ...

Oh dear, I'm sorry to say that it looks like that's just the tip of the iceberg.

Anon

Doctor Doctor, all of my relationships with unemployed people have failed ...

What, have none of them worked?

Andrew Madden

Doctor Doctor, I keep thinking I'm a caterpillar ...

Don't worry, you'll soon change.

Anon

Doctor Doctor, I'm unhappy with your service so I'm seeing a doctor in Mexico ...

Oh, you've crossed the border now.

Andrew Madden/Anon

Doctor Doctor, I can't help thinking I'm a goat ...

How long have you felt like this?

Since I was a kid.

Anon

Doctor Doctor, I'm afraid of hurdles...

Don't worry, you'll get over it.

Anon

Doctor Doctor, Aaa, Eee, I, oooh, You
...

I think you may have irritable vowel
syndrome.

Anon

Doctor Doctor, everyone keeps calling me the party mushroom ...

You must be a fun-gi.

Andrew Madden/Anon

Doctor Doctor, I have a big problem, please help me out ...

Certainly. Which way did you come in?

Anon

Doctor Doctor, I think I'm turning into an apple ...

Don't worry, I'm sure we'll get to the core of it.

Andrew Madden/Anon

Doctor Doctor, I think I'm suffering from deja vu ...

Didn't I see you yesterday?

Anon

Doctor Doctor, I've become invisible ...

Sorry, I can't see you right now.

Andrew Madden/Anon

Doctor Doctor, I think I have Tom Jones syndrome ...

It's not unusual.

Anon

Doctor Doctor, I can't stand sitting ...

No-one can.

Andrew Madden

Doctor Doctor, I keep comparing things with something else ...

Don't worry, it's only analogy.

Anon

Doctor Doctor, my teeth are very sensitive ...

OK. I'll try not to upset them

Andrew Madden

Doctor Doctor, the woman waiting after me said you had become a vampire ...

Necks please.

Andrew Madden/Anon

Doctor Doctor, I decided to have that brain operation ...

Oh, did you change your mind?

Andrew Madden

Doctor Doctor, I've got amnesia ...

Just go home and try to forget about it.

Anon

Doctor Doctor, you say the universe is made up of neutrons, protons, electrons ...

And morons now you're here.

Andrew Madden/Anon

Doctor Doctor, I keep thinking I'm a moth ...

I'm a doctor, not a psychiatrist.

I know, but I was passing by and your light was on.

Anon

Doctor Doctor, I'm in a jam ...

Oh, do you want some butter with it?

Andrew Madden

Doctor Doctor, will this cream clear up my spots? ...

Possibly, but I never make rash promises.

Anon

Doctor Doctor, that medicine you gave me for my Miley Cyrus obsession is rubbish ...

Why? Is it not twerking?

Andrew Madden

Doctor Doctor, I keep spots before my eyes ...

Have you seen a doctor recently?

No, just spots.

Anon

Doctor Doctor, I think I'm the god of love ...

Oh, don't be cupid!

Andrew Madden/Anon

Doctor Doctor, when I stand up quickly I keep seeing Mickey Mouse, Goofy and Pluto ...

How long have you been having these disney spells.

Anon

Doctor Doctor, I can't stand my job on the drilling site ...

Oh, is it a boring job?

Andrew Madden/Anon

Doctor Doctor, I've broken my arm in two places ...

Well, I wouldn't go back to either of those places if I were you.

Anon

Doctor Doctor, last week I fell into an upholstery machine ...

Oh, are you fully recovered?

Andrew Madden/Anon

Doctor Doctor, I feel like a pony ...

Neigh problem. You're just a little hoarse.

Anon

Doctor Doctor, I hate my job at the bakery but I can't quit ...

Why's that?

I kneed the dough.

Anon

Doctor Doctor, I'm afraid of Father Christmas ...

I think you're suffering from Claustrophobia.

Anon

Doctor Doctor, every time I act in the theatre I feel like I'm falling through the floor ...

Don't worry, it's just a stage you're going through.

Andrew Madden/Anon

Doctor Doctor, I swallowed a fish bone ...

Are you choking?!

No. I really did!

Anon

Doctor Doctor, I believe that I'm the monsoon king ...

How long have you rained?

Andrew Madden

Doctor Doctor, I've got a strawberry stuck in my ear ...

Don't worry, I've got some cream for that.

Anon

Doctor Doctor, I hear that you're very popular with your patients ...

Yes, people are dying to come and see me.

Andrew Madden

Doctor Doctor, I keep thinking I'm a dog ...

Well, just sit down on the couch and we'll talk it through.

But I'm not allowed to sit on the couch!

Anon

Doctor Doctor, I keep thinking I'm a toilet ...

Yes, you do look a little flushed.

Andrew Madden

Doctor Doctor, I envisioned that today would be Armageddon ...

Sorry I have little time today. Come and see me tomorrow.

Andrew Madden

Doctor Doctor, I feel like my brain's exploding ...

Don't worry, it's all in your head.

Andrew Madden

Doctor Doctor, I'm suffering from insomnia ...

Try sleeping right on the edge of the mattress. You'll soon drop off.

Anon

Doctor Doctor, I feel like a snail with no shell ...

Yes, you are acting a little sluggish.

Andrew Madden

Doctor Doctor, what's the quickest way to get to hospital? ...

Just lie in the road outside.

Anon

Doctor Doctor, I believe that I'm a fountain pen ...

Hahaha! Please stop, or I'll be inklined to leak myself.

Andrew Madden

Doctor Doctor, I've only got 59 seconds to live ...

Just a minute please.

Anon

Doctor Doctor, I had ebola this morning ...

Really? Ebola?!

Yes, e-bola cornflakes.

Andrew Madden/Anon

Doctor Doctor, I heard that exercise kills germs. Is it true? ...

Possibly, but how do you get the germs to exercise?

Anon

Doctor Doctor, I really disliked the idea of having a beard ...

But you have a beard now.

Yes, it gradually grew on me.

Andrew Madden/Anon

Doctor Doctor, I've gone all crumbly like a cheese biscuit ...

You're crackers.

Anon

Doctor Doctor, I keep thinking I'm a tree stump ...

Don't worry, we'll get to the root of the problem.

Andrew Madden/Anon

Doctor Doctor, I want a second opinion ...

OK. Come back tomorrow.

Anon

Doctor Doctor, I believe that I'm a large male cow in a salad bowl ...

Well, that's a load of bull for starters.

Andrew Madden

Doctor Doctor, I like wearing a suit and sitting in a tree ...

Are you a branch manager?

Andrew Madden/Anon

Doctor Doctor, everybody thinks I'm a liar ...

Well, I find that a little difficult to believe.

Andrew Madden

Doctor Doctor, I swallowed a roll of film ...

Take these, have a good sleep, and then see how it develops.

Anon

Doctor Doctor, HELP ME RIGHT NOW!
I KEEP THINKING I'M A DOG! ...

Okay, okay! No need to bark at me.

Andrew Madden

Doctor Doctor, I feel like a pair of curtains ...

Oh pull yourself together!

Anon

Doctor Doctor, in autumn the trees always harass me ...

Oh, how so?

They just won't leaf me alone.

Andrew Madden

Doctor Doctor, I've been unable to drink my medicine after my bath as you instructed ...

Oh? Why not?

Well after drinking my bath I've got no room left for medicine.

Anon

Doctor Doctor, I've swallowed a pen ...

Well sit down on the desk and write your name.

Anon

Doctor Doctor, I need a cure for my sleepwalking ...

Try these, sprinkle them on the floor before you go to bed.

Is it a special kind of medicine?

No, they're drawing pins.

Anon

Doctor Doctor, I feel like an old tree ...

Don't cedar to these feelings, it's pine. To me you'll always be evergreen.

Andrew Madden

Doctor Doctor, how do I stop my foot running? ...

Stick your foot out and trip it up.

Anon

Doctor Doctor, my wife is a cow who just won't shut up! ...

Just tell her to stop yakking.

Andrew Madden

Doctor Doctor, I feel like a pack of cards ...

I'll deal with you later.

Anon

Doctor Doctor, my wife is a horse and just won't take no as an answer ...

Just tell her neigh means neigh.

Andrew Madden

Doctor Doctor, I've got amnesia ...

When did this begin?

Anon

Doctor Doctor, I can't believe I'm a sheep! ...

What will it take to ram it home? Ewe'll have to believe it eventually.

Andrew Madden

Doctor Doctor, I lost my job at the fountain pen patenting firm ...

Oh why's that?

They said I was the source of the leaks.

Andrew Madden

Doctor Doctor, I'm being taken to court by some atoms ...

Don't worry, most judges know that they make up everything.

Andrew Madden/Anon

Doctor Doctor, over the years as a soldier I've experienced mustard gas and pepper spray attacks ...

Wow, you sound like a seasoned veteran.

Andrew Madden

Doctor Doctor, I just can't put a price on this flavour ...

Well, there's no accounting for taste.

Andrew Madden

Doctor Doctor, I look like a beggar and smell like a fish ...

What a poor sole.

Andrew Madden

Doctor Doctor, I tried to catch some fog this morning ...

Really? What happened?

Well, my memory's a bit hazy, but I think I mist.

Andrew Madden/Anon

Doctor Doctor, part of me feels like a cat and nobody trusts me anymore ...

Yes, you do look like a bit of a cheetah.

Andrew Madden

Doctor Doctor, my nose is bleeding ...

Did you pick your nose?

No, I was born with it.

Andrew Madden

Pirate Doctor Doctor, bin got a headache, gift me some pills ...

Sorry, I ain't.

Why that be?

Because the parrots-ate-em-all.

Andrew Madden/Anon

Pirate Doctor Doctor, I ain't learn th' alphabet ...

Why's that?

I be stuck at 'C' for months.

Andrew Madden/Anon

Doctor Doctor, I'm really good at sleeping ...

How do you figure that?

I can do it with my eyes closed.

Andrew Madden/Anon

Doctor Doctor, I think I'm Dracula ...

Oh God, not you again! You're a real pain in the neck!

Andrew Madden

Doctor Doctor, I wish I had a dollar for every time a girl has said I'm unattractive ...

Why's that?

Because then I'd be attractive.

Andrew Madden/Anon

Doctor Doctor, this medicine for my skepticism really works? ...

Really? Are you sure?

Andrew Madden

Doctor Doctor, I think I'm a whiteboard ...

That's remarkable.

Anon

Doctor Doctor, I had some serious beef with my wife yesterday ...

Why's that?

She's a vegetarian.

Andrew Madden

Doctor Doctor, last night my wife told me I was self-centered for eating all the shrimps ...

Yes, you do look a little shellfish.

Andrew Madden

Doctor Doctor, a cheese board blew up in my face yesterday ...

Are you OK?

Well, I was hot by a piece of de-Brei.

Let me take a look …

I was feeling a little Blue, but now I'm feeling much Feta.

Andrew Madden

Doctor Doctor, I feel like a muffler ...

Yes, you look exhausted.

Andrew Madden/Anon

Doctor Doctor, I'm so worried about my husband, he thinks he's an injured grape ...

Oh? Why's that?

Every time he goes to the toilet he lets out a little wine.

Andrew Madden

Doctor Doctor, I have a bladder infection ...

Sounds like urine trouble.

Andrew Madden/Anon

Doctor Doctor, I'm so happy to be a cake ...

What does your wife think about this?

She's so happy to be a cake too. At our wedding we were in tiers.

Andrew Madden/Anon

Doctor Doctor, I keep having a dream about swimming in an ocean of ornge soda...

It's just a fanta-sea.

Anon

Doctor Doctor, I slept like a log last night ...

So why did you come to see me?

I woke up in the fireplace.

Andrew Madden

Doctor Doctor, I'm worried. I think I'm a calendar ...

Why worried?

My days are numbered.

Anon

Doctor Doctor, I think I'm telepathic ...

Yes, I know.

Andrew Madden

Doctor Doctor, I'm quitting my job as a can-crusher ...

Why's that?

It's soda-pressing.

Andrew Madden

Doctor Doctor, I'm afraid of touch screen technology ...

Afraid of what exactly?

I'm not sure. I just can't put my finger on it.

Andrew Madden/Anon

Doctor Doctor, I just can't go on thinking I'm a bike ...

Why's that?

I'm two tyred.

Andrew Madden

Doctor Doctor, I've started devil-worshipping ...

For what reason?

Nothing really. Just for the hell of it.

Andrew Madden/Anon

Doctor Doctor, I think I'm a piece of thin paper ...

Oh that's tearable.

Anon

Doctor Doctor, my wife says I'm average ...

Don't worry, she's just being mean.

Anon

Doctor Doctor, I found new employment getting paid to sleep ...

Sounds like a dream job.

Anon

Doctor Doctor, I'm addicted to the hokey-pokey ...

Don't worry, we'll soon turn you around.

Andrew Madden/Anon

Doctor Doctor, I had to turn down that job inspecting mirrors ...

Why's that?

I just couldn't see myself doing it.

Anon

Doctor Doctor, I have limited vocabulary ...

How limited?

Words can not express it.

Anon

Doctor Doctor, people say I have no empathy ...

You shouldn't care what they think.

Andrew Madden/Anon

Doctor Doctor, my grandmother had diarrhea, my mother had diarrhea, and now I have diarrhea ...

It looks like it runs in your jeans.

Andrew Madden

Doctor Doctor, I have kleptomania ...

You should take something for it.

Andrew Madden/Anon

Doctor Doctor, I'm going to shoot your family, frame them, and them hang them from the walls of your home ...

What?! Who are you?!

I'm the photographer. I thought we had an appointment?

Andrew Madden/Anon

Doctor Doctor, I'm afraid of elevators/lifts ...

Well, you'll have to take steps to avoid them.

Andrew Madden/Anon

Doctor Doctor, I hate Russian dolls ...

Yes, they're so full of themselves aren't they.

Andrew Madden/Anon

Doctor Doctor Frankenstein, don't you ever get lonely? ...

No, I'm good at making friends.

Andrew Madden/Anon

Doctor Doctor Watson, do you know another name for tummy-button? ...

Erm, naval?

Belly-entry my dear Watson.

Andrew Madden

Doctor Doctor, I've gone to the gym for ten years ...

Oh, don't you want to go home?

Andrew Madden

Doctor Doctor, My husband always gave 100% no matter what he was doing ...

Oh, how did he die?

Giving blood.

Andrew Madden/Anon

Doctor Doctor, everyone is so condescending to me ...

You do know what condescending means don't you?

Andrew Madden

Doctor Doctor, I only drink a little, but when I do, I turn into a different person ...

And why's that a problem.

That person drinks a lot.

Andrew Madden

Doctor Doctor, I'm annoyed, you did that massage on me incorrectly ...

Oh, sorry to rub you up the wrong way.

Andrew Madden/Anon

Doctor Doctor, I hate life after I got a universal remote control ...

Why's that?

Well, it changed everything.

Andrew Madden

Doctor Doctor, I'm always flying in my dreams as Peter Pan ...

What? You Neverland?

Andrew Madden

Doctor Doctor, I've swallowed some scrabble tiles ...

Whatever you do don't go to the toilet or it could spell disaster.

Andrew Madden/Anon

Doctor Doctor, I used to be addicted to soap ...

Are you clean now?

Anon

Doctor Doctor, I want to marry my wifi ...

Why's that?

We just have a great connection.

Andrew Madden

Doctor Doctor, my eye-trouble got me fired from my job at school ...

Oh? Why?

I couldn't control my pupils.

Andrew Madden/Anon

Doctor Doctor, a book fell on my head ...

Well, you've only got your-shelf to blame.

Andrew Madden/Anon

Doctor Doctor, did you hear? All the toilets in town have been stolen ...

Oh! Have the police got anything to go on?

Andrew Madden/Anon

Doctor Doctor, I feel like a small horse ...

How long have you felt like this?

Oh, donkey's years.

Andrew Madden

Doctor Doctor Lector, why didn't you eat your ex-wife? ...

She was very bitter.

Andrew Madden/Anon

Doctor Doctor Lector, I heard you prefer eating readers to writers ...

Yes, writers cramp but readers digest.

Andrew Madden/Anon

Doctor Doctor, people keep ignoring me ...

Andrew Madden

The Naughty Bits

Doctor Doctor, I keep thinking I'm the child of a tree ...

Oh God, you really are a son of a birch!

Andrew Madden

Doctor Doctor, I swallowed a model of the solar system ...

Don't worry, just bend over and let's see if Uranus pops out.

Andrew Madden

Doctor Doctor, I think that I'm a big pile of dung ...

Pffft. What a load of crap.

Andrew Madden

Doctor Doctor, my midget husband dies of excitement ...

Oh yes, he does look like he's a little stiff.

Andrew Madden

Doctor Doctor, I've got a cricket ball stuck up my bottom ...

How's that?!

Anon

194

Doctor Doctor, my wife told me sex is better on holiday ...

Oh yes, she sent me a postcard too.

Andrew Madden/Anon

Doctor Doctor, every time I strip to my underpants I imagine I'm a 6 foot 11 fortune teller ...

So, a large medium in smalls.

Andrew Madden

Doctor Doctor, I really can't eat nuts ...

Oh? Why's that?

Every time I come to eat them, I just don't have the balls.

Andrew Madden

Doctor Doctor, when in fancy dress as a pirate I had a terrible vision about my future wife ...

Really? What about her exactly?

A sunken chest with no booty.

Andrew Madden/Anon

Doctor Doctor, I've got really bad BO ...

Oh, do you want to try this ball deodorant?

Erm, no. Something for my armpits would be better.

Andrew Madden/Anon

Doctor Doctor, I've got a pain in me groin ...

That's because you've got a steering wheel down your pants.

Aye, it's drivin' me nuts.

Andrew Madden/Anon

Doctor Doctor, I want to complain about the cost and quality of my circumcision ...

What about it?

It was a rip-off.

Andrew Madden

Doctor Doctor, I get really excited when reading books ...

Well, you probably should stop touching your shelf.

Andrew Madden

Doctor Doctor, I farted and accidentally followed through whilst in the elevator/lift ...

That crap's just wrong on so many levels.

Andrew Madden

Doctor Doctor, I'm trying to stay away from Jazz and Classical music ...

Yes, too much sax and violins can only lead to treble.

Anon

Doctor Doctor, I can't forget the image of my ex-girlfriend sitting on the toilet ...

Ah yes, this is your number two girl friend, right?

Yes, it's all such a mess. I stool can't forget her feces.

Andrew Madden

Doctor Doctor, I was constipated recently ...

Oh really? You don't seem too concerned.

Well, I couldn't really give a crap.

Andrew Madden

Doctor Doctor, I can't really measure how effective that Viagra you gave me has been ...

Here's a ruler.

Andrew Madden

Doctor Doctor, socially, my job at the sewage treatment plant is terrible ...

Why's that?

I get a lot of crap from my friends.

Andrew Madden/Anon

Doctor Doctor, the lawyer for my trial on kerb-crawling charges was wonderful ...

Oh, did he help you get off?

Andrew Madden

Doctor Doctor, I have five penises ...

Oh, your underwear must fit like a glove.

Andrew Madden/Anon

Doctor Doctor, I like wearing my wife's mini-skirt in public ...

Wow. That really shows you've got balls.

Andrew Madden/Anon

Doctor Doctor, every day, I run home
and rip off my wife's bra ...

Oh really?

Yes, it really chafes my nipples.

Andrew Madden

Doctor Doctor, my girlfriend started smoking ...

Well, maybe next time use some lubricant.

Andrew Madden/Anon

Doctor Doctor, I have a premature ejaculation problem ...

When did it start?

I don't know it just came out of nowhere

Andrew Madden/Anon

Doctor Doctor, I have a really bad masturbating habit ...

Don't worry, eventually we'll beat it together.

Andrew Madden

Dedication

This book is dedicated to a father and to a son. A father, who is sadly no longer with us, would have been driven absolutely crazy by the punny nature of this book, as my general humour generally did to him when he was with us. But as one life ends, another begins. I can only hope that I don't drive my son crazy too.

I'd also like to make a special dedication to Anon, as without him/her, this world would feel like an empty place ...

One more, to laughter. As laughter brings a smile to peoples' faces. Namely your own.

Andrew Madden

www.doctordoctorjokes.com

The Official Books

www.theofficialbooks.com

37845353R00130

Printed in Great Britain
by Amazon